Planning and Goal Setting for Improved Performance Participant's Guide

Contributing Authors

Alan King

Bob Oliver

Bob Sloop

Kelly Vaverek, Ph.D.

Series Editor

Esther Safir Powers, Ph.D.

Sponsoring Editor: Jim Sitlington
Developmental Editor: Custom Editorial Productions
Production Editor: Holly Terry
Production House: Custom Publishing Services
Internal Design: Ellen Pettengell Design
Cover Design: Joseph M. Devine
Marketing Manager: Stephen E. Momper

I(T)P
International Thomson Publishing
Thomson Executive Press (a division of South-Western College Publishing) is an ITP Company. The trademark
ITP is used under license.

1 2 3 4 5 MZ 9 8 7 6 5
Printed in the United States of America

ISBN No. 0-538-84362-4

Acknowledgements

My sincerest thanks to Alan King, Bob Oliver, Bob Sloop, and Kelly Vaverek, Ph.D. for their generous contributions to this book, as well as to Esther Safir Powers, Ph.D., for her tremendous work both as contributing author and series editor.

—Michael H. Mescon, Ph.D.
The Mescon Group, Inc.

Contents

Introduction to *Planning and Goal Setting for Improved Performance*   3

Self-Awareness Tool: How Do You Prefer to Plan?   7

Information Update #1: A Primer on Planning   11
    Review Questions   15

Information Update #2: Setting and Achieving Worthwhile Goals   19
    Review Questions   21

Information Update #3: Action Planning   27
    Review Questions   37

Application Questions   41

Action Plans   55

Evaluation Form   73

Introduction to Planning and Goal Setting for Improved Performance

Introduction to *Planning and Goal Setting for Improved Performance*

The *Performance Through Participation*™ Series (PTP) helps build successful, participative organizations. It provides the knowledge, skills, and abilities you and your fellow employees will need to create a culture that values contribution from everyone.

Planning and goal setting is the foundation for organizational success. It is the road map to our productivity. When we plan, the future is less likely to take us by surprise and force us into a difficult situation. Planning reduces the time we spend putting out fires and increases our ability to prevent them. Planning gives us control.

This module contains:

▲ An introduction

▲ A self-awareness tool: "How Do You Prefer to Plan?"

▲ Three information updates to broaden and deepen your knowledge of the topic:

- A Primer on Planning

- Setting and Achieving Worthwhile Goals

- Action Planning

▲ Information review questions to check your understanding of the updates

▲ Application questions to help you apply your new knowledge

▲ Action plans to help you put into practice today, what you have learned

Planning and Goal Setting for Improved Performance Goals

Planning and Goal Setting provides productive steps for improving performance goals. By participating actively in this module, you will learn:

▲ The principles of planning and goal setting

▲ How to plan and set goals at work

▲ What tools to use to make planning more effective

Planning and Goal Setting for Improved Performance Objectives

In *Planning and Goal Setting for Improved Performance*, you will discuss key concepts, real situations in which they are applied, and how to apply them at work. You will then be ready to try out these ideas. Specifically you will be able to:

- ▲ Describe what a plan is
- ▲ Explain why plans are important
- ▲ Identify the key elements of the planning process
- ▲ Evaluate the soundness of a plan
- ▲ State the characteristics of an effective goal
- ▲ Describe the goal-setting process
- ▲ Discriminate between effective and ineffective goal statements
- ▲ Create an action plan
- ▲ Use planning and goal setting with your work group

Your Role

While completing the self-awareness tool and reading information updates, keep the module's goals and objectives in mind. Ask yourself, "What kinds of goals does my work group or team have?" "Who sets the goals?" "Are there clear plans for reaching important goals?" "How can my work group or team and I set goals and design plans more effectively?"

To get the most out of *Planning and Goal Setting for Improved Performance*, prepare for the session by completing the self-awareness tool, reading the information updates, and completing the review questions. Focus on the information presented, participate in the discussions, speak your mind freely, listen thoughtfully to others, and implement the action plans to try out new behaviors.

Self-Awareness Tool

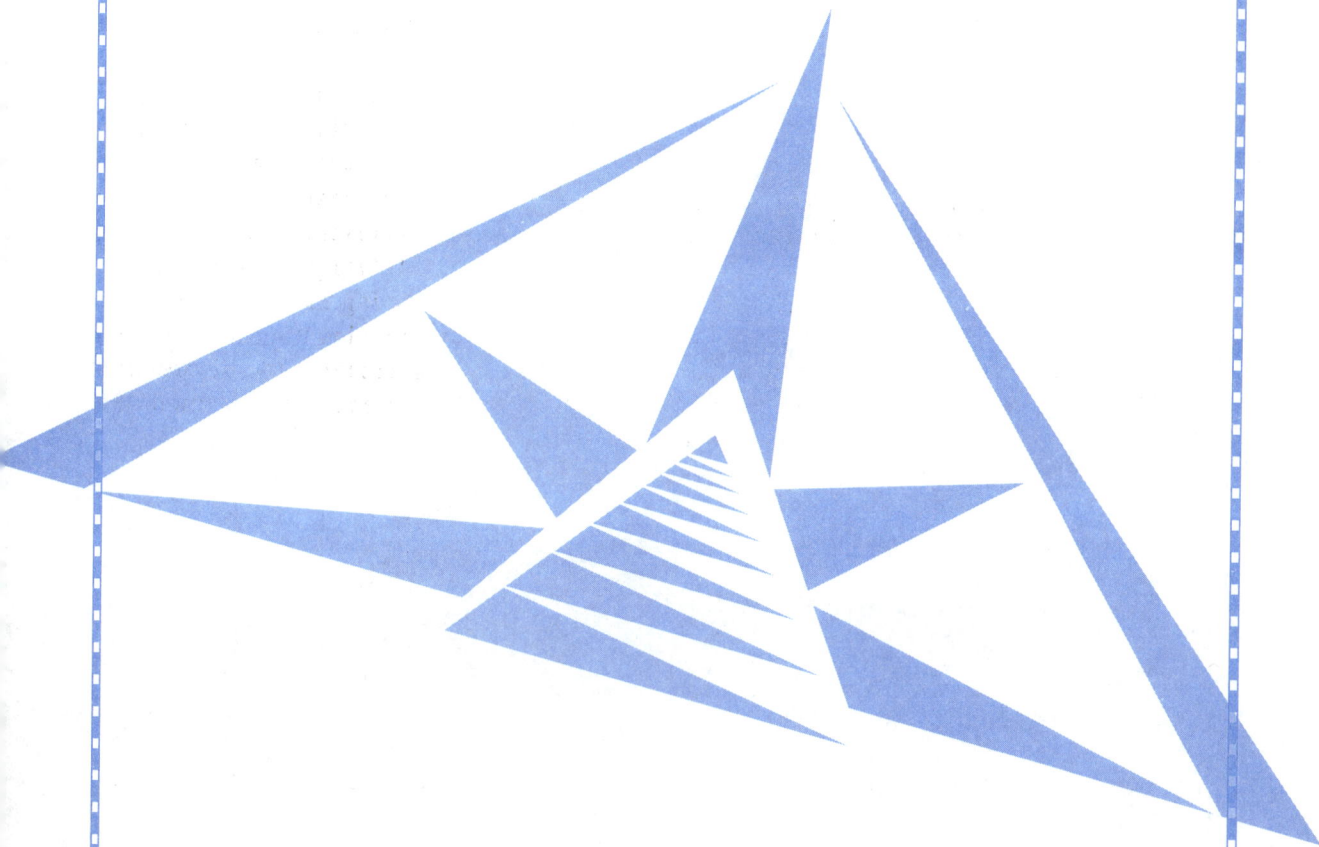

Self-Awareness Tool

Directions: For each of the following pairs of statements, select the item that best describes what you usually do. Then put the item letter in the space provided. At the end, you will be able to determine your planning preference.

_____ 1. a. When change is coming, I think ahead of time how to best prepare for it.
   b. I prepare for change when it is happening. By then I have more information.

_____ 2. a. Planning involves going off by yourself and thinking.
   b. Planning involves meeting with people to exchange thoughts and ideas.

_____ 3. a. A goal should be specific and have a fixed completion date.
   b. A goal is a broad statement about our direction.

_____ 4. a. A sound plan considers all the possible changes that can affect the outcome and includes multiple contingencies.
   b. A sound plan is a living, dynamic management tool and should be flexible.

_____ 5. a. Planning never stops.
   b. Planning is a specific activity that takes place just before a change, an assignment, or a project.

_____ 6. a. If the people above you don't plan, it's impossible for you to plan.
   b. If the people above you don't plan well, it's especially important to plan carefully.

_____ 7. a. In effective companies, some people plan and other people carry out the plan.
   b. In effective companies, everyone plans.

_____ 8. a. Planning and goal setting are so interrelated that they are sometimes confused.
   b. Planning and goal setting are distinct, separate activities.

_____ 9. a. If someone says to you, "I need this by Tuesday, with no errors, for less than $500," there is still a need for significant planning.
   b. If someone says to you, "I need this by Tuesday, with no errors, for less than $500," the planning has been done.

_____ 10. a. Setting goals beyond people's grasps gives them that extra push for excellent results.
   b. Setting reachable goals produces the best results.

SCORING

1 — a	6 — b
2 — b	7 — b
3 — a	8 — a
4 — b	9 — a
5 — a	10 — b

INTERPRETATION

Check your responses against those listed above. Where you disagree, you'll find that this module will help to think about the issue in a new way. If you found a choice difficult, this module will help to clarify your understanding about planning and goal setting. If you found the choices easy, congratulations—you have a solid, basic understanding of the subject. This module will help you fine-tune your knowledge and skills.

A Primer on Planning

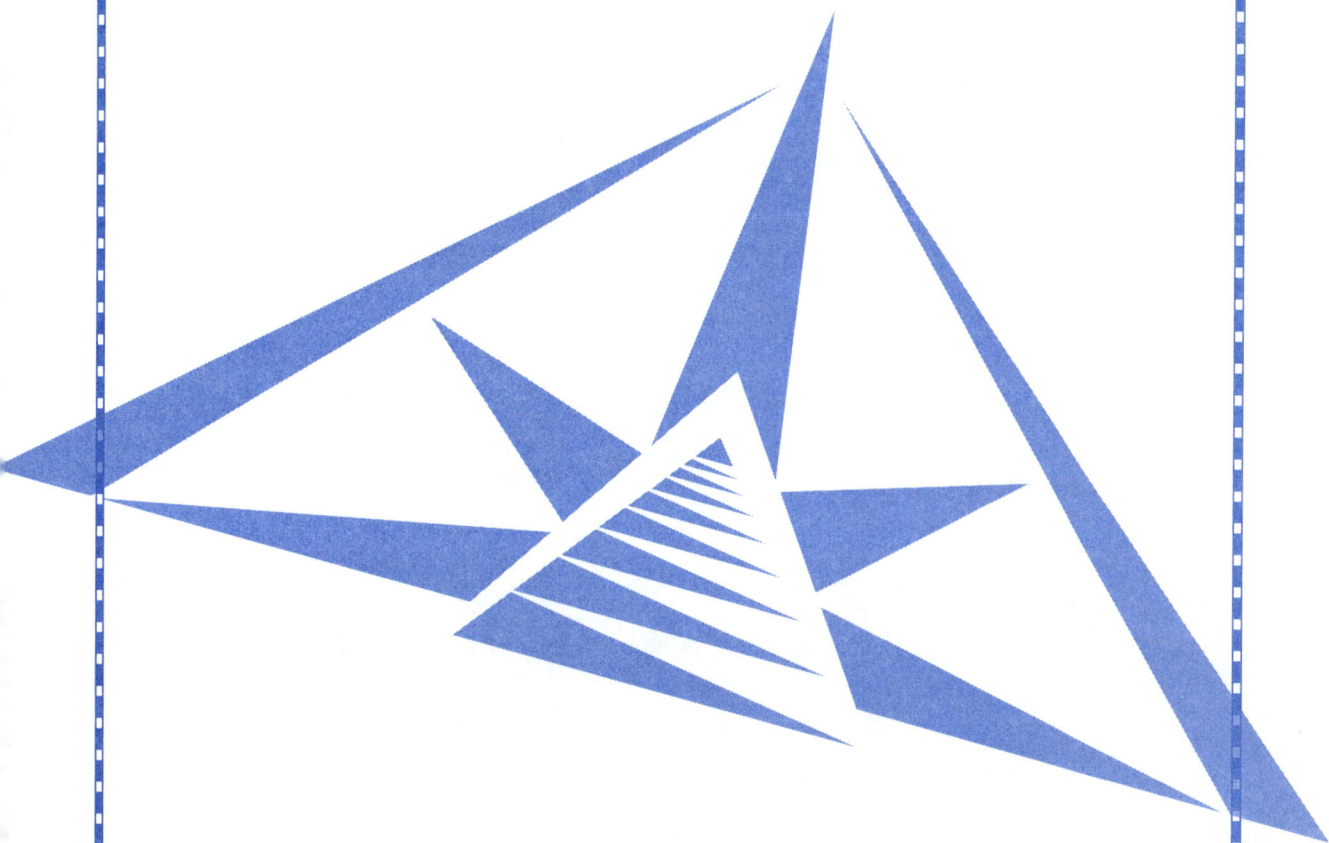

A Primer on Planning

To plan or not to plan;
Not only is that not the question
That is no longer even an option!

INTRODUCTION

The statement above could well have been uttered by today's prototypical middle manager. Managers today simply *must* plan. Without plans (even mediocre ones) the modern corporate ship quickly finds itself adrift—directionless and foundering—at the mercy of stormy seas, shifting tides, and multitudinous customers and stockholders. None of whom is all that *pleased* with the way their ship is being run.

One of the few truths of management states, "*When you fail to plan, you plan to fail.*" A cliche? Yes...but like most clichés, it also happens to be true.

A plan is a document which sets forth the resources (people, finances, authorizations, time), contingencies, and actions required to achieve an identified goal. Planning is the basis for action, which should always consider present realities as well as what is likely to happen. This produces the context within which planning takes place. It should never be attempted in a vacuum, ignoring the activity within a company or a business unit.

WHAT IS A PLAN?

There are many kinds of plans developed in today's corporate environment:

▲ Business plans   ▲ Marketing plans   ▲ Advertising plans

▲ Promotional plans   ▲ Financial plans   ▲ Operating plans

▲ Distribution plans   ▲ Employee plans   ▲ Succession plans

A plan is like a road map. It shows where we are now (the present context, today's state of the company or business unit), where we want to go (the goal), and how to get to the destination (strategy and tactics). Like a map, a good plan shows key landmarks (milestones/checkpoints) along the route so that we can check our progress. If a milestone/checkpoint doesn't show up when it should, we're off course and need to take corrective action to get back on track.

In planning a trip we recognize that detours around known problems (road construction, for example) will be necessary. Instead of being surprised by the detours, we determine how to accommodate them before setting out on the journey. The same is true for planning within an organization. Enroute to the goal of a plan, we have to accommodate problems and determine (in advance) how to solve them.

Before setting out on a trip, we must estimate the needed resources and support. How much will the journey cost? Do we fly or drive? Will we need relief drivers along the way?

A good plan contains similar estimates before its inception. If the plan appears to be too costly, at least three choices appear: modify the plan, increase its funding, or abandon the plan until appropriate funding levels become available.

Enlisting active support for a plan is just as important as calculating and allocating for its likely cost. Planning should never be attempted in a vacuum and never be attempted alone. To make a plan successful, involve those who will implement it, those who must approve it, and those who will be affected by the plan. The earlier we get them involved in the planning process—enlisting their ideas and suggestions—the more they will take "ownership" of the resulting plan and work actively for its successful completion.

Good plans are essential tools with which organizations can improve themselves and their results. If a plan doesn't support an organization's work strategies as well as its values, direction, and needs, then it's not a plan at all. It's merely an expensive diversion in terms of time and effort.

TIME FRAMES FOR PLANNING

Plans sometimes fail because planners don't choose the appropriate time frames for different types of plans.

Strategic Plans

Strategic plans are detailed, comprehensive, and integrated long-range plans to ensure that an organization meets its mission and objectives. Strategic plans are usually formulated by top management, but their execution requires the efforts of people at all levels of the organization. They are blueprints that guide firms for extended periods—usually one to five years. The effects of strategic plans often are not realized for several years.

Tactical Plans

Tactical plans support strategic plans. They are the "how to do" counterpart to the strategic plan's "what to do." Usually devised for a period of a year or less, their results are evident shortly after they are implemented. If the results are slow or off-target, tactical plans are quickly revised to achieve the desired effect in the near term. Tactical and strategic plans must be aligned to achieve the organization's desired results.

Rules of Thumb   To give a plan its best chance for success...

▲ Involve all those who will be affected by the plan in its formulation.

▲ Invite their input and involvement from the beginning of the planning process.

▲ Communicate the plan widely—both up and down the organization.

▲ Make the plan flexible. A good plan is a living, dynamic management tool. If something goes awry, be ready to revise strategies or to quickly change tactics.

▲ Measure the plan's progress. Determine a reasonable, achievable timetable. If interim target dates can't be met, change the plan or extend its completion date.

▲ Regularly report the plan's progress to all those involved.

THE PLANNING PROCESS

The Seven Steps of the Planning Process

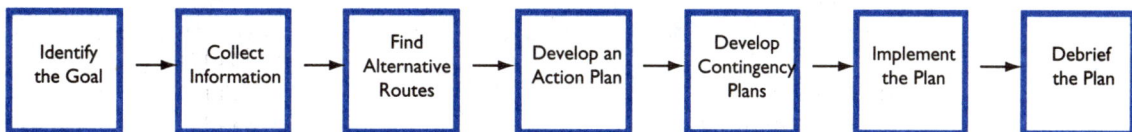

| Identify the Goal | → | Collect Information | → | Find Alternative Routes | → | Develop an Action Plan | → | Develop Contingency Plans | → | Implement the Plan | → | Debrief the Plan |

Good planning requires sound, logical thinking and reasoning. It is a dynamic process to achieve a definite, measurable goal while continually asking, "What if?" The following are the seven steps of the planning process.

1. Identify the goal of the plan—a quantifiable improvement in quality or service, a specific sales increase, a measurable improvement in plant maintenance.

2. Collect information about the current reality and the desired condition which a plan is designed to produce. Consider the current status of all appropriate levels of the organization, including your company, your division, and your primary work unit. Describe this context in simple terms. If this context changes, your plan will also have to change. Collect information about future events for your work group. Describe this in realistic terms. Anticipate the important threats that may prevent your group (and your company) from reaching the goal of the plan.

3. Find several alternative routes to accommodate both threats and opportunities that may arise. Choose the alternatives which have the

best chance of succeeding, then evaluate the advantages and disadvantages of each. Consider all the resources (finances, people, authorizations, time) that each alternative requires. Identify the roadblocks—such as a budget cutback—that may prevent the achievement of each option.

4. Develop an action plan by establishing sub-goals or interim checkpoints and the timetable for each. An action plan includes specific activities, the responsible individual, completion dates, resource requirements, and milestones/checkpoints. Action plans determine what needs to be done, by whom, and by when, to get planners from where they are—to where they want to be. Set a completion date for the entire plan. Make sure it's realistic and achievable. (Constructing action plans will be discussed further in Information Update #3.)

5. Develop contingency plans for dealing with unexpected positive and negative events.

6. Implement the plan. At regular intervals, communicate the plan's progress to people at all appropriate levels of the organization. Remain flexible and be prepared to change direction to respond to problems, opportunities, and changes in the context in which the plan was devised. When the plan is complete and the goal achieved, communicate your success and reward those who contributed.

7. Debrief the plan, determine why it succeeded, share what you've learned, and plan actions for improving the process next time.

ATTRIBUTES OF A SUCCESSFUL PLAN

The planning process produces the basis for action. For that action to be appropriate, timely, and targeted, consider a plan in light of these questions:

- ▲ Is it clear? Do those who must approve and implement the plan understand it?
- ▲ Does the plan agree with the values and purpose of the company, division, and work unit?
- ▲ Does it deal effectively with both threats and opportunities?
- ▲ Are the plan's goals specific, measurable, and reasonably achievable?
- ▲ Is the plan a true basis for action?
- ▲ Have adequate resources been allocated to support it?
- ▲ Are responsibilities for individual efforts clearly described and assigned?

- ▲ Does the plan anticipate unforeseeable events? Are there contingency plans?

- ▲ Are interim checkpoints clearly established? Who reports these? How? To whom?

- ▲ Is the plan flexible enough if events warrant a change? Will you know if such change is needed?

Even a poor plan is better than no plan at all. Poor plans can be improved if their progress is evaluated regularly and realistically.

Using the process described on the preceding pages planners can work their way through a plan's deficiencies and improve it "on the run." However the best plans are dynamic and flexible. They have alternatives built into them to accommodate changes in both the organization and in those who must authorize, implement, and support the plan.

WHY PLAN?

Planning is the basis for action. In today's business environment, there simply is no other choice. Middle managers *must* plan if the organizational unit is to survive and succeed. Good planning requires the understanding and support of senior management along with enthusiastic involvement of those implementing the plan. Plans should never be devised for their own sake. If there is no compelling reason to create a plan, it is not needed. Planning time can better be used in other, more productive pursuits. At the same time plans should not sit on a shelf for months, only to be used at a performance review. Sound, effective planning may at first seem difficult and demanding. However with practice it can—and should—become an indispensable management tool.

Review Questions

Most managers agree that planning is important. But they tend to respond to a situation as it arises rather than actually plan for it. They complain that time pressures and other circumstances make it difficult to plan effectively.

1. What is planning? How do you create a plan?

_____

_____

_____

_____

_____

2. Why is planning important?

_____

_____

_____

_____

3. What are the characteristics of a sound plan?

_____

_____

_____

_____

Setting and Achieving Worthwhile Goals

Setting and Achieving Worthwhile Goals

"If you don't know where you're going...any bus will take you there!"

INTRODUCTION

Like the passenger with no destination, no plan is meaningful without a goal, a destination toward which the plan is aimed. Goals give our lives—and our businesses—direction and purpose. Worthwhile goals also introduce discipline and self-management. These are powerful resources for making sound plans and staying the course to achieve those goals.

GOALS AND THE PLANNING THAT FOLLOWS

In military terms, a goal is the objective of any exercise. Plans are the tactics and strategy—the "how to do it, and how to get there." Plans are the means by which goals are realized.

And while some find that goal-setting is much easier than planning, goal-setting is nonetheless essential to the success of any enterprise. Without knowing where we're going, we'll never get *anywhere*, never achieve anything of real worth.

SETTING GOOD GOALS

What *is* a good goal? How do we know when a goal is both achievable and worthy of our best efforts? It is said that the best goals are... S-M-A-R-T! This is an acronym to remember that goals should be:

Specific, **M**easurable, **A**ttainable, **R**ealistic and **T**imely.

Here are some good and bad examples of each attribute:

Specific:　　Not general

Poor example—Improve quality.

Good example—Assembled products will be 99.5% error-free by year's end.

Measurable:	Quantifiable
	Poor example—Increase sales.
	Good example—Sales revenue will improve 15% by the end of this quarter.
Attainable:	Achievable within the context of present realities
	Poor example—Double our revenues.
	Good example—Achieve 10% higher revenue within three months.
Realistic:	Capable of realization in light of existing resources
	Poor example—All employees will have perfect attendance.
	Good example—Absenteeism rate will not exceed 2% per year.
Timely:	Time by which goal must be accomplished.
	Poor example—Provide periodic updates.
	Good example—Submit operating results daily by close of business.

Subgoals

It is important to remember that establishing a single, overall goal is seldom sufficient for good business planning. Subgoals give us checkpoints along the way to the goal's achievement and help us stay on track.
Here's an example:

Goal:	Decrease next year's computer downtime by 20%.
Subgoal:	All group members will complete a half-day course on troubleshooting software problems by May 1. Tom, Dick, and Harriet will study service delivery issues and present their recommendations for improvements by March 1.
Goal:	Increase sales calls to customers by 15% over the previous year's number.
Subgoal:	Hire five more account representatives before June 1 and include customer visitation frequency in revised annual review for all reps.

Whatever the number of goals, be careful about setting too many or too few. Too few goals may focus efforts too narrowly—leaving significant performance areas unattended. Too many goals can dilute focus and energy or create goal conflicts.

Departmental, unit, or team goals should align closely with the goals of the corporation or the larger organization of which the department, unit, or team is a part.

Goal setting must always be done in the context of both present realities and future possibilities. Goal setting involves predicting which events, policies, and people (both inside and outside an organization) are likely to influence their success or failure. Ask questions like these:

▲ What is the direction of the corporation? Are our goals consistent with that?

▲ Will the goals we're setting keep us aligned with corporate policy and priorities?

▲ What is the competition doing? How are their activities likely to impact our goals?

▲ What pending government policies (tax changes, regulatory revisions) are likely to influence our goals and our plans for achieving them?

To ignore such matters is to be ostrich-like and naive in our goal setting. While it takes work to evaluate potential actions by competition and various levels of government, enlightened goal setting is a payoff that makes the effort well worthwhile.

GETTING EVERYONE "ON BOARD"

How does the savvy manager ensure that one's peers and subordinates enthusiastically support and work hard in pursuit of their group's goals? By simply enlisting their involvement in actually setting the goals. Employees who've had a hand in establishing goals are considerably more likely to "get on board" with the plans. Employees involved in the setting of goals not only know where they're going, they also know the right bus to take to get there. Given the chance, they'll even help *drive* the bus to the destination.

Review Questions   Goal setting is a critical step in planning. The goal setting process can improve the effectiveness of work groups in many ways.

1. What part does goal setting play within the planning process?

_____

_____

_____

2. Why should team members be involved in setting or finalizing goals which will affect them?

_____

_____

_____

3. For each of the following statements, identify whether the goal is S-M-A-R-T.

▲ Customer service will be improved.

_____

_____

_____

▲ Production volume will increase 17%.

_____

_____

_____

▲ Area 3 will reduce its reject (defect) rate by next month.

_____

_____

_____

▲ All individuals should have plans for self-development.

_____

_____

_____

Beginning June 30, updated inspection standards will be completed and in use by teams.

_____

_____

_____

Information Update #3
Action Planning

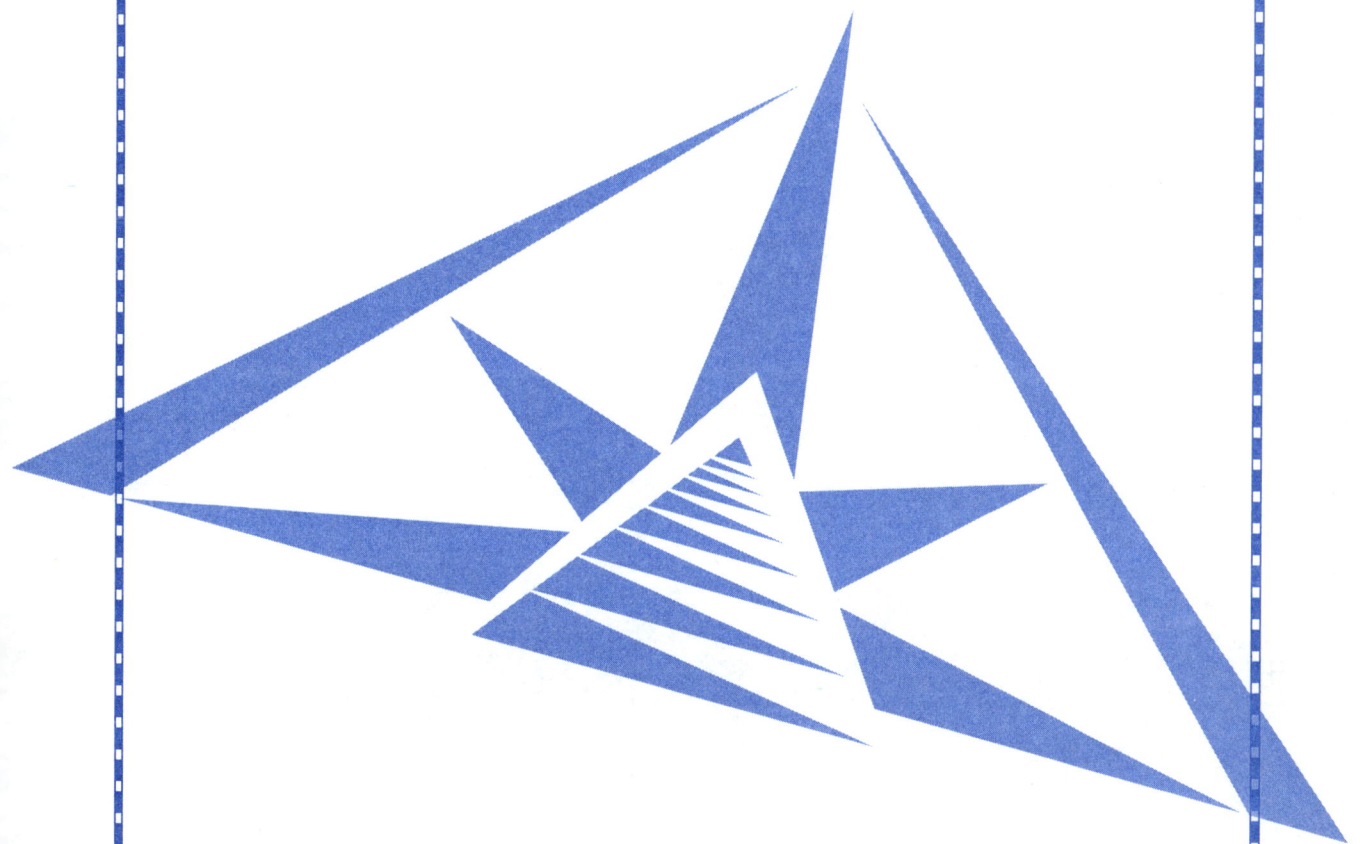

Action Planning

After reading Information Updates #1 and #2, you now understand how vital planning and goal setting is to an organization. You understand the Seven-Step model in the planning process and you have learned how to identify S-M-A-R-T goals. Now that we know where we want the organization to go, how do we actually get there? We need to construct an action plan.

An action plan contains all the elements necessary to bring the goal of the plan to reality. These elements include identification of specific activities, the individual or group responsible for each activity, resource requirements, completion dates, and the milestones/checkpoints along the way to the plan's completion.

An action plan answers the questions:

▲ What must be done? (Event/Task)

▲ By whom? (Primary person responsible)

▲ With what? (Resources needed)

▲ By what dates? (Target completion date)
   ... to move us from where we are to where we want to be.

Action planning tools are all around us. Sometimes we take them for granted because we use them every day:

▲ A clock tells us how much production time remains in the day.

▲ A calendar tells us when to plan our summer vacation schedules.

▲ A slip of paper reminds us of things we must accomplish before week's end.

▲ A telephone call produces information for submitting an order for new materials.

▲ A brief meeting reveals the need to schedule overtime for the coming week.

1. ***Identify Specific Tasks.*** If your goal is to increase sales for your territory (or business unit) by 20 percent within the first two quarters of next year and an additional 10 percent by year's end, there will be a number of activities necessary to achieve that goal. You may need to hire additional staff (Who? By what date? At what cost?). You may need to adjust pricing (By what amount? Do you have the authority to do this? Who does?). In answering these questions and others, you will be able to determine the specific tasks to increase sales.

2. ***Divide the Job—Who is Responsible for Each Task?*** In evaluating the skills and people required to complete an action plan, consider the following:

   ▲ Who has the necessary skills?

   ▲ Who has demonstrated experience?

   ▲ Who is presently available to work on the project?

   ▲ Who would benefit by the experience of working on it?

   It's usually a mistake—especially in crisis projects—for managers to try to handle most of the work themselves.

3. ***Procure Resources to Get the Job Done.*** In virtually every action plan, we have to compare the resources needed for the project versus those that are immediately available. The difference between the two reveals the resources that must be procured to successfully complete the assignment. Usually these resources fall into four categories: people, money, time, and materials/equipment.

4. ***Schedule the Project's Steps and Set Completion Dates (Interim and Final).*** Scheduling means planning the times at which specific milestones or checkpoints should occur. Before you can begin scheduling these you must make a list of the events and processes necessary to reach the goal.

5. ***Review Progress: Milestones and Checkpoints.*** In formulating your action plan, determine when—at which critical points—you will follow up on the plan's progress. This doesn't mean casually asking, "How's it going?" It means formally following up with those who are actually working to implement the plan. What are their problems? Their needs? Their anxieties? Are they on time and on course? The manager's role is to monitor the plan, make any required changes, and offer assistance to attain the goal.

Gantt charts are useful for organizing projects and for communicating key events as a project continues.

There are four major steps to creating a Gantt chart:

1. Identify the necessary steps.

2. Estimate the start and stop time for each step, as well as the duration of each step in days, weeks, or months.

3. Assign responsibility for each step.

4. Graph the steps on a time line.

To illustrate the creation of a Gantt chart, let's look at the series of sequential steps (simplified here for ease of presentation) required to build a home:

1. Grade

2. Build and pour foundation

3. Frame house

4. Wire house

5. Install plumbing

6. Install drywall and interior trim

7. Install exterior siding and trim

8. Landscape

9. Paint interior

10. Paint exterior

As the illustration on page 31 shows, building a house consists of the 10 sequential tasks identified above and will take 64 work days or almost 13 weeks (See Duration column of figure). This time period may or may not be acceptable. If a competitor can complete the same house more quickly, or the buyer needs the house before the projected completion date, then a more condensed construction schedule must be considered.

Note that start and finish dates are given for each of the steps, as well as a sequencing of steps in the Preceding Steps column. The Resource column assigns responsibility for each step. Finally, a bar graph visually depicts the information in the Gantt chart.

PERT (Program Evaluation Review Technique) charts grew out of the need for control of more complex projects that began to occur during the space age. Gantt charts are fine for initial project planning and communication of general project information. Many projects become complex with several interdependent elements that must be coordinated to complete a project on time and within budget.

Normally, PERT charts are used as the primary control tool for complex projects. PERT charts take at least twice the time to complete as Gantt charts.

To complete a PERT chart, one follows the first three steps of a Gantt chart and then four additional steps:

First three steps of the Gantt chart:

1. Identify the necessary steps.

2. Estimate the start and stop time for each step, as well as the duration of each step in days, weeks, or months.

3. Assign responsibility for each step.

    Four additional steps:

4. Determine the interrelationship between the various steps.

5. Graph the steps showing their relationship.

6. Determine the project's critical path of activities.

    Critical path activities determine the minimum time to complete the project.

7. Optional. Each step can be allocated a "slack time" or time to spare before it affects the critical path.

The PERT chart on page 32 illustrates the house-building example. Note that all of the steps are considered critical and no optional slack times are provided.

Gantt Chart for Building a House

ID	Name	Duration	Scheduled Start	Scheduled Finish	Preceding Steps	Resources
1	Grade	4d	11/21/94	11/24/94		Evergreen Grading & Landscaping
2	Build & Pour Foundation	8d	11/25/94	12/6/94	1	Benny Johnston Foundations
3	Frame the House	9d	12/7/94	12/19/94	2	Thomas Framing
4	Wire the House	6d	12/20/94	12/27/94	3	Vogel Electrical
5	Install Plumbing	7d	12/28/94	1/5/95	4	Whitlow Plumbing
6	Install Drywall & Interior Trim	6d	1/6/95	1/13/95	5	Robert's Trimworks
7	Install Exterior Siding & Trim	9d	1/16/95	1/26/95	6	Covington Siding Co.
8	Landscape	4d	1/27/95	2/1/95	7	Evergreen Grading & Landscaping
9	Paint Interior	5d	2/2/95	2/8/95	8	Homeplace Painting Co.
10	Paint Exterior	6d	2/9/95	2/16/95	9	Homeplace Painting Co.

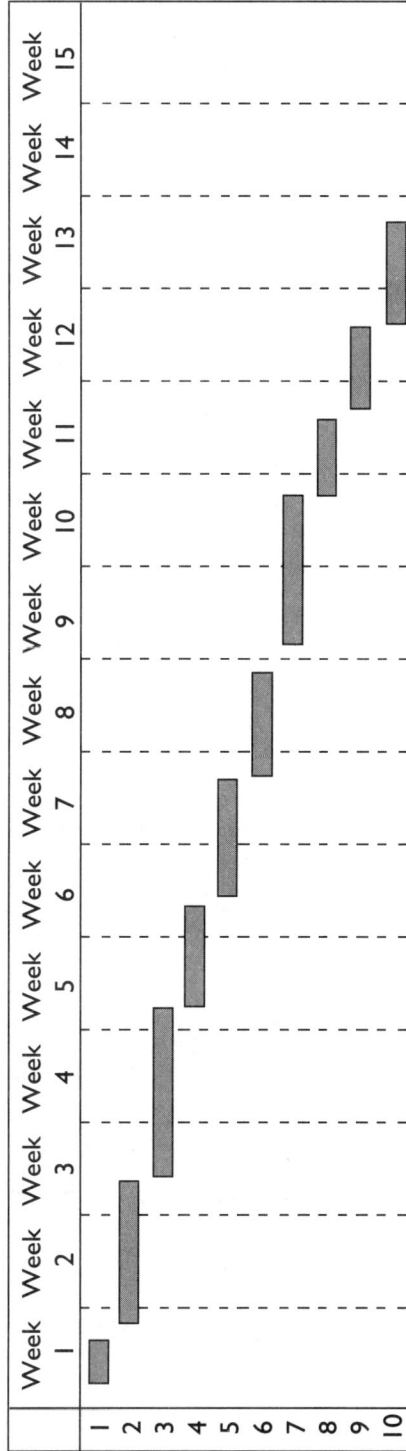

PERT Chart for Building a House

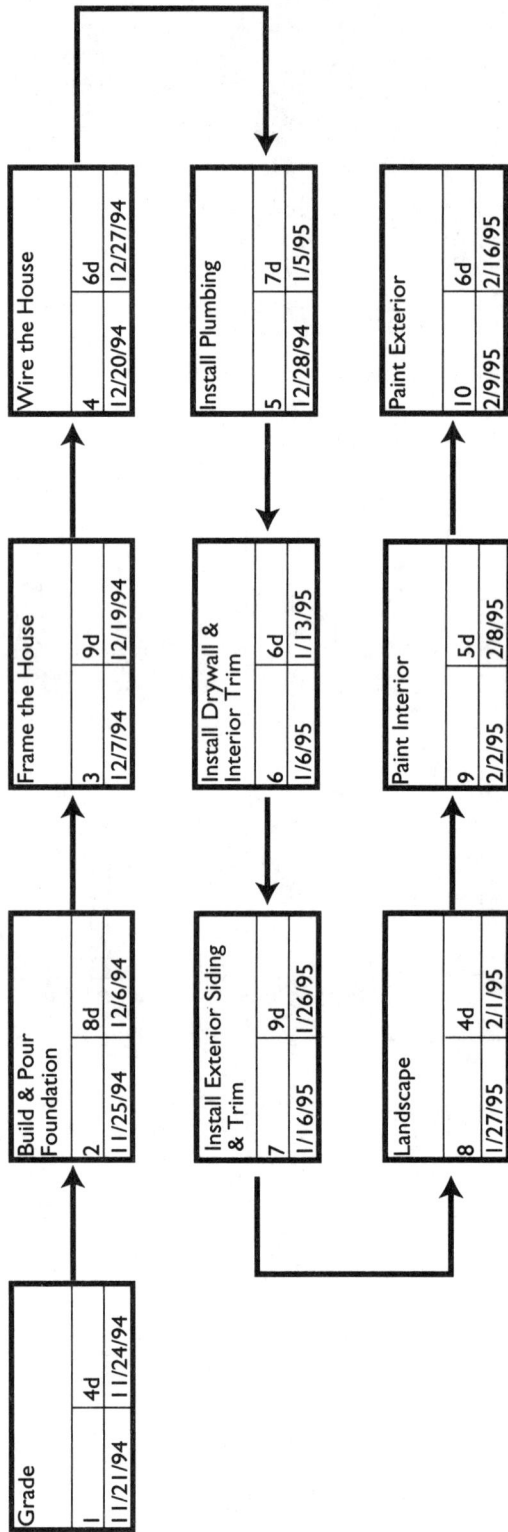

Grade		
1	4d	11/24/94
11/21/94		

Build & Pour Foundation		
2	8d	12/6/94
11/25/94		

Frame the House		
3	9d	12/19/94
12/7/94		

Wire the House		
4	6d	12/27/94
12/20/94		

Install Plumbing		
5	7d	1/5/95
12/28/94		

Install Drywall & Interior Trim		
6	6d	1/13/95
1/6/95		

Install Exterior Siding & Trim		
7	9d	1/26/95
1/16/95		

Landscape		
8	4d	2/1/95
1/27/95		

Paint Interior		
9	5d	2/8/95
2/2/95		

Paint Exterior		
10	6d	2/16/95
2/9/95		

Key:

Critical

Noncritical

Name		
ID	Duration	Scheduled Finish
Scheduled Start		

Now, let's say that market demand or the performance of competitors requires that we build houses faster. There are two fundamental ways to shorten project time. One way is to perform individual tasks faster. The other way is to perform sequential tasks in parallel. It would be hard to frame a house before the foundation is complete using common construction techniques. With some inconvenience and coordination, one could, however, complete plumbing and wiring at the same time.

Some tasks, such as internal painting and external painting, are often done sequentially because the same contractor uses the same crew to do both. Using different crews or even different contractors on the two painting tasks would allow the steps to be completed independently of one another.

The Gantt and PERT charts on pages 34–35 show which steps in our house-building example can be combined as parallel activities in order to "shrink" project time. The revised plan creates a more complex schedule, but the completion time is cut from 64 work days to 43 workdays or 9–10 weeks.

The critical path is the *sequence* of steps that must be completed in order to finish a project in the least amount of time. Adding the length of time on the critical path steps results in the minimum project time. Steps 1, 2, 3, 5, 7, and 10 are the critical path steps in our example. The work days needed to complete these steps are 4, 8, 9, 7, 9, and 6 days respectively, or 43 work days total. Every day of delay in completing one of these critical path steps will add a day to the project.

Note in this revised schedule that four steps are considered noncritical: wire the house, install drywall and interior trim, paint interior and landscape. These activities are considered noncritical because the length of time to complete them does not impact the project completion time. For example, wiring the house could be delayed one day without changing the completion date because plumbing is being done at the same time and it takes longer. Both plumbing and wiring have to be done before the next steps (exterior siding and interior drywall) can be started. Neither can be started until the framing is complete.

These four noncritical activities all have built in slack time. They can be delayed without changing the project completion date. For example, landscape (Step 8) has two days of built-in slack time because landscaping can be started at the same time as exterior painting (Step 10) but completed two days sooner. This means that if landscaping activities are delayed for up to two days, the project can still be completed on time.

Gantt and PERT charts, though sometimes tedious to design, are excellent action plans. With a Gantt and PERT chart in hand, it becomes considerably easier to budget a project, monitor its progress, and anticipate problem areas. Many computer software programs are available today to assist in the development of both kinds of charts.

Revised Gantt Chart for Building a House

ID	Name	Duration	Scheduled Start	Scheduled Finish	Preceding Steps	Resources
1	Grade	4d	11/21/94	11/24/94		Evergreen Grading & Landscaping
2	Build & Pour Foundation	8d	11/25/94	12/6/94	1	Benny Johnston Foundations
3	Frame the House	9d	12/7/94	12/19/94	2	Thomas Framing
4	Wire the House	6d	12/20/94	12/27/94	3	Vogel Electrical
5	Install Plumbing	7d	12/20/94	12/28/94	3	Whitlow Plumbing
6	Install Drywall & Interior Trim	6d	12/29/94	1/5/95	4,5	Robert's Trimworks
7	Install Exterior Siding & Trim	9d	12/29/94	1/10/95	4,5	Covington Siding Co.
8	Landscape	4d	1/11/95	1/16/95	7	Evergreen Grading & Landscaping
9	Paint Interior	5d	1/6/95	1/12/95	6	Homeplace Painting Co.
10	Paint Exterior	6d	1/11/95	1/18/95	7	Homeplace Painting Co.

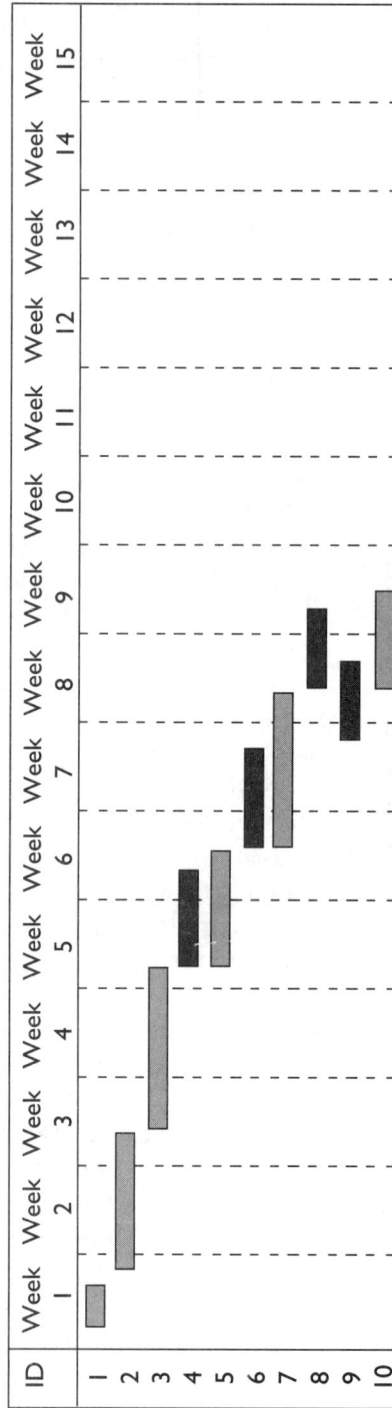

ID	Week 1	Week 2	Week 3	Week 4	Week 5	Week 6	Week 7	Week 8	Week 9	Week 10	Week 11	Week 12	Week 13	Week 14	Week 15

Key: Critical ▮ Noncritical ▯

Revised PERT Chart for Building a House

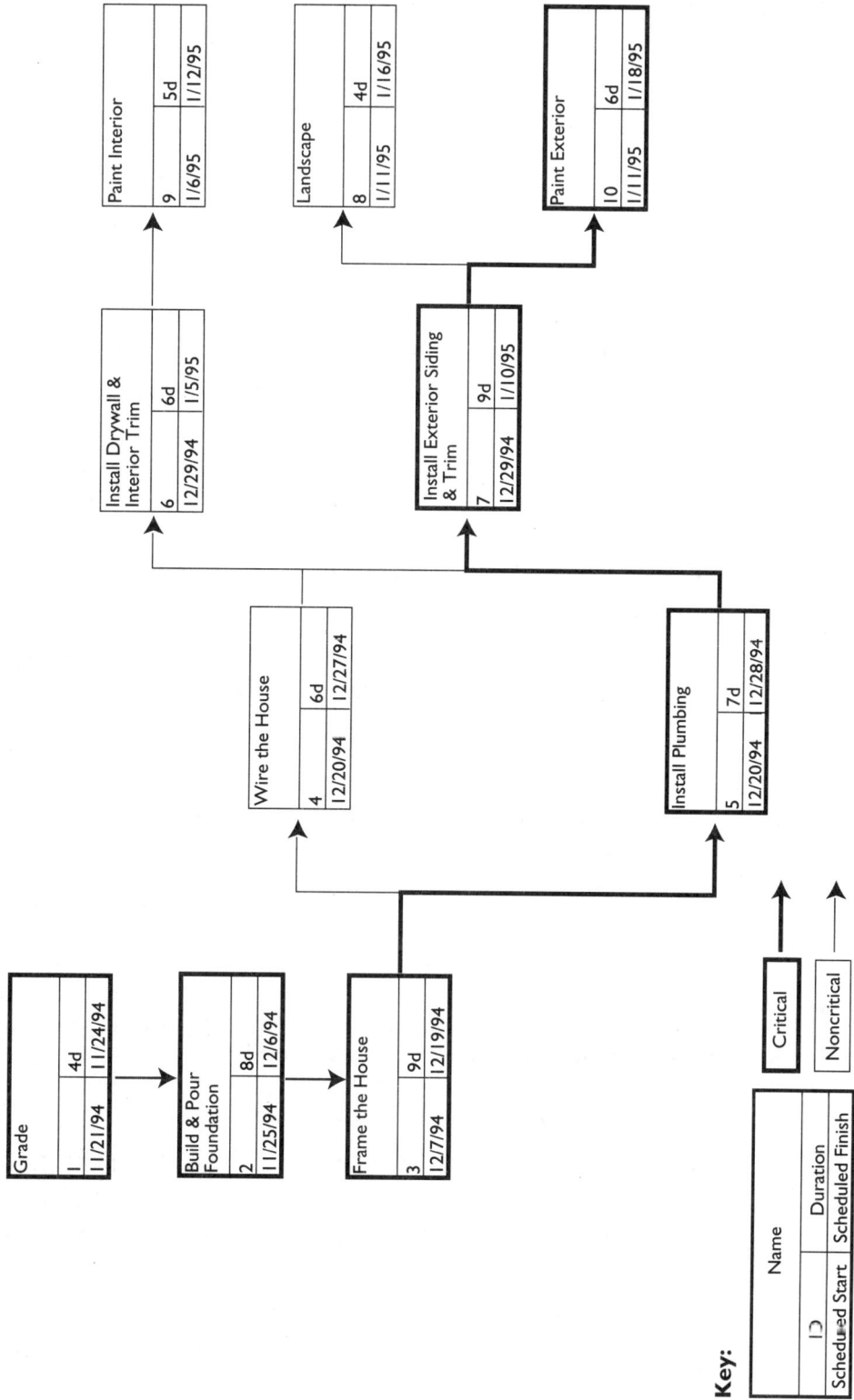

Grade		
1	4d	
11/21/94		11/24/94

Build & Pour Foundation		
2	8d	
11/25/94		12/6/94

Frame the House		
3	9d	
12/7/94		12/19/94

Wire the House		
4	6d	
12/20/94		12/27/94

Install Plumbing		
5	7d	
12/20/94		12/28/94

Install Drywall & Interior Trim		
6	6d	
12/29/94		1/5/95

Install Exterior Siding & Trim		
7	9d	
12/29/94		1/10/95

Paint Interior		
9	5d	
1/6/95		1/12/95

Landscape		
8	4d	
1/11/95		1/16/95

Paint Exterior		
10	6d	
1/11/95		1/18/95

Key:

Critical

Noncritical

Name		
ID	Duration	
Scheduled Start		Scheduled Finish

"Something is always waiting to go wrong." (Also known as Murphy's Law: *"If something can go wrong, it will."*)

Corollary #1: What will go wrong will be what you least expect.

Corollary #2: It will hit harder than you ever thought possible.

Developing Contingency Plans

Contingencies are events which may or may *not* happen. Contingency planning simply means preparing for eventualities which are different from those we expect.

Contingency planning is a skill that saves sweat, tears...and careers. Contingency planning means anticipating the unexpected. Here are some tips for improving your success at looking ahead:

▲ Invite those with appropriate practical experience to join you in a meeting.

▲ Without group discussion, ask each person to write down the most likely contingencies for your project. (You'll benefit from the individual assessment of each "expert" without prior input from the group.)

▲ Ask each attendee to describe their contingencies.

▲ Invite the group to discuss each contingency.

▲ After this discussion, ask the group to vote on the most likely contingencies, how to plan for them and how to work around them.

Not every contingency merits a detailed backup plan. Remember to involve others who are experienced in your type of project or assignment in your contingency planning. Good contingency planning is based on the highest quality information and input available.

Implement the Plan

Though some view planning as a lonely intellectual activity, it doesn't have to be. First, good planning actively involves those who will be needed to implement the formulated plan. Second, planning can be a satisfying, highly visible, and exciting process. Third, good planning always involves good communication...up and down the organization. Some guidelines for communicating the plan include:

▲ Let others know of changes that affect the plan.

▲ Communicate progress and motivate others to continue giving their best.

▲ Continue to solicit others' ideas, responses, cooperation, and feedback.

▲ Get agreement on and negotiate options.

▲ Ask for information from people who have special knowledge or experience in the subject of your project.

Debrief the Plan   When the plan has been completed, evaluate the results against the goal originally set. If it didn't achieve everything it was designed to achieve, determine what went wrong, why, and how a similar problem can be avoided in the future. Communicate the completion and achievements of the plan to others within your company and work unit. Be certain to praise those who contributed to its conclusion.

ACTION PLANS: THE ESSENTIAL MANAGEMENT TOOL

Let's imagine that after the successful Allied invasion of Europe at Normandy, France, on "D-Day" (June 6, 1944), the man who had directed that unprecedented military operation was asked if everything had gone the way it was supposed to go. Dwight D. Eisenhower, then Supreme Allied Commander and later President of the United States, could have made the following observations:

"No, not exactly. The weather had been rotten the day before with heavy seas and rain. But, we got a break in that weather and we went in. Many of our paratroopers, jumping in darkness early that morning, landed miles from their intended targets and didn't get into the fight for days afterward. Some landed in the middle of enemy troops and lost their lives needlessly. Because of heavy tides, one whole element of our amphibious naval assault missed their assigned beach by miles and had to fight their way up high cliffs against dug-in, withering enemy firepower. No, things didn't exactly go the way they were supposed to go. But, we had a *plan*. And we had planned for many of the contingencies we faced that day. We knew what we had to do, and we did it—pretty much according to plan. That plan plus the dedicated and heroic people who carried it out made all the difference. The D-Day plan was, literally, the difference between life and death; the difference between our victory and defeat."

Good planning? It makes all the difference in the world!

Review Questions   Everyone—managers, team members, staff—can plan more effectively by developing simple action plans.

1.   What questions does an action plan answer?

_____

_____

_____

_____

2. What are the five steps to developing an action plan?

_____

_____

_____

_____

_____

Application
Questions

Application Questions

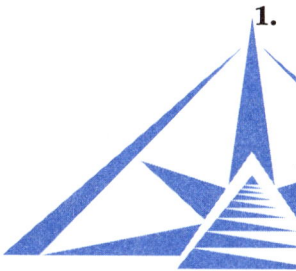

1. ***Maria's Goals.*** JETCO's vision is to become the preferred provider of commercial jet engines to airframe manufacturers. Last year each senior executive interviewed a customer. They learned that customers consider JETCO's engines "top of the line." Quality is high. JETCO corrects any problems efficiently and effectively. The customer's biggest concern is the time to get an order delivered (cycle time), sometimes as long as 24 months. The senior executives decided that this year's priority is cutting cycle time from order placement to delivery by half.

   Maria is the gearbox area team leader. The gearbox includes the gear system, starter, and lubrication pumps. Maria set several goals to boost the team's performance. The goals include:

   ▲ Increase output by 10% by December 31

   ▲ Decrease the rejection rate by 14% by December 31

   ▲ Reduce overtime by 500 hours by December 31

   Maria believes that all three goals can be met. As a working member of the team, she knows the group and its problems. She didn't talk with anyone about the goals. Maria held a group meeting to announce the goals. There was little discussion, so she assumed everyone understood the goals and knew what to expect. A month has passed since the meeting. It has become obvious that actual results are nowhere near the goal levels.

   a. What are some problems with Maria's goal-setting process?

   _____

   _____

   _____

   _____

b. How should the team goals be changed to better support JETCO's vision?

_____

_____

_____

_____

c. What should Maria do to improve the goal-setting process?

_____

_____

_____

_____

2. **_Harry's Aggressive Goals._** Harry is a firm believer in pushing his team's performance to the limits. He sets high goals for himself, and the goals he sets for the team far exceed what can be achieved. Harry works hard and helps the team, but the goals are rarely achieved. "Sometimes you win and sometimes you don't, but people need something to shoot for," Harry says.

   a. What do you think of Harry's goal-setting approach? Explain.

   _____

   _____

   _____

   _____

   b. What are the effects of individuals and teams continually failing to achieve their goals?

   _____

   _____

   _____

   _____

   c. What can happen when goals are always set below people's ability to perform?

   _____

   _____

   _____

   _____

3. ***Hiring Time at the Firm.*** Ed is the managing partner for a 150-person law firm. The firm specializes in employment and labor law. Business is booming and the partners have just authorized Ed to hire 25 entry-level lawyers during the next five months.

Ed is proud of his planning skills. He knows a S-M-A-R-T goal when he sees one, and the new hire goal is S-M-A-R-T. Ed knows that to hire 25 lawyers, he has to:

▲ Determine what kinds of lawyers are needed by talking to other lawyers in the firm (2 days)

▲ Go to college campuses to recruit (1 month)

▲ Have candidates complete application forms (3 weeks)

▲ Check the candidates' references (5 days)

▲ Interview the candidates to prescreen (6 weeks)

▲ Schedule on-site interviews between the screened applicants and other lawyers in the firm (5 days)

▲ Extend and negotiate employment offers (1 month)

▲ Complete the paperwork on the new hires (4 days)

Ed knows that once he gets the plan in place, nothing will deter him from getting those new hires.

a. Develop a Gantt chart for Ed's process, using the time frames given.

Gantt Chart for Application Question #3: Hiring Time at the Firm

Step	Action Item	Time (Days)	Start	Finish	Preceding Step	Resource
1						
2						
3						
4						
5						
6						
7						
8						

Step	Action Item	Feb	Mar	Apr	May
1					
2					
3					
4					
5					
6					
7					
8					

b. What are the critical points in Ed's process?

_____

_____

_____

_____

c. The law firm frequently takes on large cases that completely consume all the available resources. A big case hit two months into Ed's plan. It is consuming much of Ed's and the other lawyers' time. What does this do to Ed's plan?

_____

_____

_____

_____

4. **Alicija's Plan.** Alicija is the new manager of a work group that has always performed well. The group members understand their jobs and manage their work with few problems. However the group has never had formal goals or plans. When Alice suggested that the group begin to set goals and make action plans, people hesitated. "We're doing good work, aren't we?" one person said. Another complained, "That takes too much time. Work keeps me too busy to plan." "Complicated paperwork!" commented another. "No one reads and uses those planning forms anyway."

a. Why should the team plan if it is already working well?

_____

_____

_____

b. How can the team plan if everyone is too busy working?

_____

_____

_____

c. Do goal setting and planning require complicated paperwork?

_____

_____

_____

_____

5. **Too Many Goals?** Members of Everett's team work well together and enjoy challenges. The team recently started monthly planning meetings. Team members have suggested that in addition to volume goals, quality goals, productivity goals, and attendance goals, goals should be set to improve customer service and to promote new skill development. Everett is concerned that too many goals for improvements might keep the team from meeting volume goals. Past experience indicates that top management gets more upset when production falls than about anything else.

   a. Is the team unwise to set so many goals? Explain.

   _____

   _____

   _____

   _____

   b. What planning recommendations would be helpful to this team?

   _____

   _____

   _____

   _____

6. ***The Staff Meeting.*** Every month, Joshua, the HR manager for SAFECO, and his direct reports get together for a staff meeting. Nothing seems to go right at these meetings. The only thing set in advance is the time and date. Even the place changes since conference room reservations aren't always made. The scurrying around for agenda items and review material is a nightmare. Oftentimes Joshua and the team are unprepared. The two-hour meeting drags on and on—sometimes as long as six hours—as people "remember" information to share and decisions to make. The team is fed up. They've decided this is a big problem and want to develop an action plan to reach their goal of "50 percent less time spent in meetings with 75 percent more decisions."

   a. Brainstorm a list of activities that Joshua and his team members need to meet their goal.

   b. Develop simple Gantt and PERT charts to plan the staff meetings.

   c. How should the team check its progress?

   _____

   _____

   _____

   _____

Gantt Chart for Application Question #6:
The Staff Meeting

ID	Name	Duration	Start	Finish	Preceding Step	Resource

Hours

ID	1	2	3	4	5	6	7	8	9	10	11	12

PERT Chart for Application Question #6:
The Staff Meeting

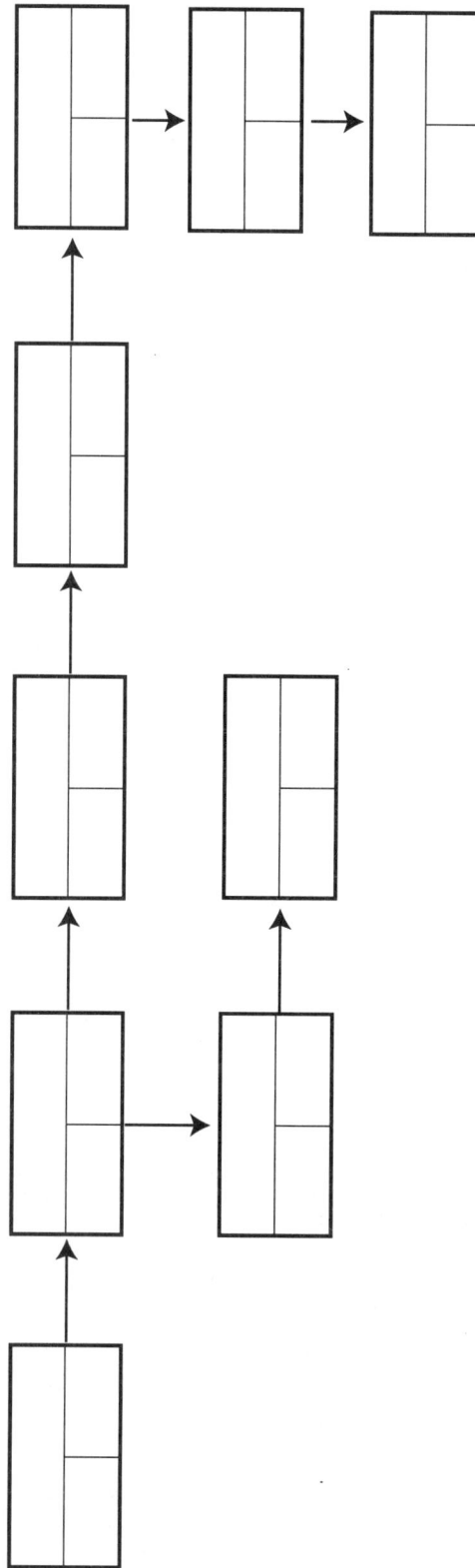

Action Plans

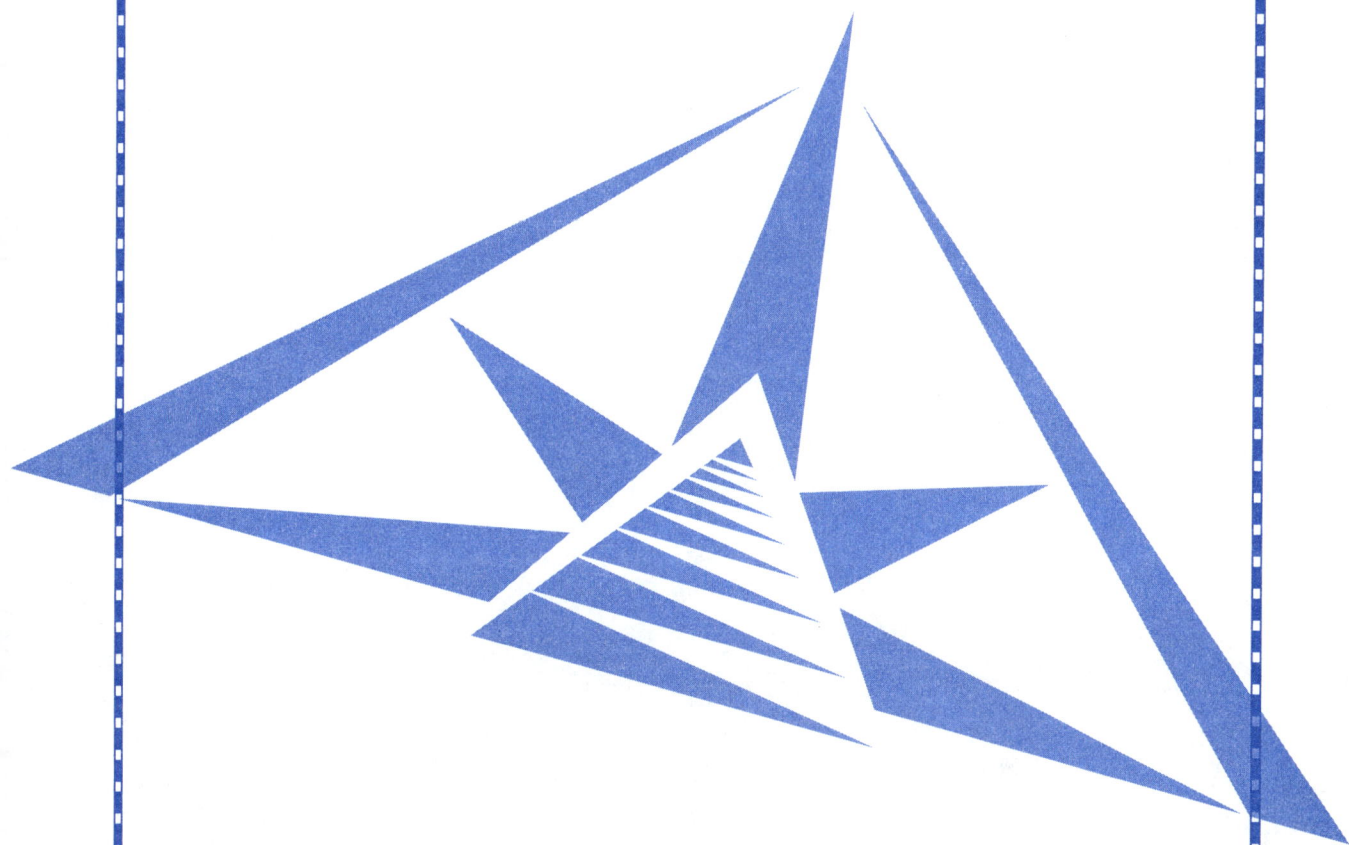

Action Plans

1. ***Your Team's S-M-A-R-T Goals.*** This action plan will help your team develop S-M-A-R-T goals.

YOUR TEAM'S S-M-A-R-T GOALS (FOR ACTION PLAN #1)

a. Record your team's goals in the space below. Don't try to make them S-M-A-R-T goals if they're not—just record them as you understand them.

1. _____

2. _____

3. _____

4. _____

5. _____

b. Using the "Assessing Team Goals" worksheet on page 57, evaluate each goal.

c. With your team, rewrite the goals so that all are S-M-A-R-T.

1. _____
   _____

2. _____
   _____

3. _____
   _____

4. _____
   _____

5. _____
   _____

Assessing Team Goals: (for Action Plan #1)

Goals are tools to communicate a purpose, explain needed results, focus efforts, and improve performance. Answer the following questions (by yourself or through team discussion) to evaluate the team's goals.

	Goal #1 Yes/No?	Goal #2 Yes/No?	Goal #3 Yes/No?	Goal #4 Yes/No?	Goal #5 Yes/No?
1. Is the goal specific?					
2. Is the goal measurable?					
3. Is the goal attainable?					
4. Is the goal realistic?					
5. Is the goal timely?					

2. ***Current Plan Review.*** This activity will help your team to determine whether its existing action plan is sound.

    a. Get out your current action plan. (Dust it off if need be.) Review the plan and reflect on how you developed it.

    b. Use the "Sound Plan Assessment" checklist on page 59 to determine its soundness.

    c. Based on your answers to the checklist, modify your existing action plan to make it more sound. An Action Plan worksheet is provided on page 60 to record your additions.

SOUND PLAN ASSESSMENT (FOR ACTION PLAN #2)

1. Is it clear? Do people understand the plan?	Yes/No
2. Does the plan agree with the values and purpose of the company, division, and work unit?	Yes/No
3. Does it deal effectively with both threats and opportunities?	Yes/No
4. Are the plan's goals specific, measurable, and reasonably achievable?	Yes/No
5. Is the plan a true basis for action?	Yes/No
6. Have adequate budget and personnel been allocated to support it?	Yes/No
7. Are responsibilities for individual efforts clearly described and assigned?	Yes/No
8. Does the plan anticipate unforeseeable events?	Yes/No
9. Arc interim checkpoints clearly established? Who reports these? How? To whom?	Yes/No
10. Is the plan flexible enough to be changed should events warrant its change?	Yes/No

ACTIVITY	RESOURCE NEEDED	DEADLINE

3. ***Personal Growth Plan.*** Planning is important for organizations, teams, and individuals. This activity will help develop an action plan for your personal growth. What do you need to do to reach your goals?

   a. Complete the "Personal Plan Development" form on pages 62–63.

   b. How will you celebrate goal attainment?

   c. Identify a time to review your progress and celebrate your success.

   d. Implement the plan.

PERSONAL PLAN DEVELOPMENT: (FOR ACTION PLAN #3)

1. *Overall Goal*

What do you want to accomplish? Where do you want to be? Write your S-M-A-R-T Goal below:

_____

_____

_____

2. *The Current Reality*

What are the opportunities and threats in your environment? What are your personal strengths and weaknesses? Fill in the squares with a description of the current reality.

OPPORTUNITIES	STRENGTHS
THREATS	WEAKNESSES

3. *Course of Action*

What path is most likely to get you to the goal?
Identify three alternatives. Select one by putting an asterisk beside it.

_____

_____

_____

4. *Develop an Action Plan*

What actions need to be taken, by when, and with what resources to implement the course of action? Complete the chart on page 64.

5. *Develop Contingency Plans*

What should I do if the situation changes? List two events that can affect your plan positively and two events that can affect your plan negatively.

POSITIVE EVENTS	NEGATIVE EVENTS

Put an asterisk beside the item that is most likely and most critical.
How will your plan change if this contingency occurs?

_____

_____

_____

_____

EVENT/TASK	RESOURCES NEEDED	TARGET COMPLETION DATE	$ BUDGETED	OTHER/NOTES

4. **Team Plans.** This action plan will help you and your team specify goals and develop a plan to accomplish those goals. It takes you through the step-by-step planning process described in Information Update #1.

   a. Complete the "Team Plan Development" form on page 66.

   b. How will the team celebrate goal attainment?

   c. Identify a time for the team to review its progress and celebrate its success.

   d. Implement the plan.

Team Plan Development: (for Action Plan #4)

1. ***Overall Goal***

   What does the team want to accomplish? Where do you want to be? Write your S-M-A-R-T Goal below:

   _____

   _____

   _____

2. ***The Current Reality***

   What are the opportunities and threats in your environment? What are your team's strengths and weaknesses? Fill in the squares with a description of the current reality.

Opportunities	Strengths
Threats	Weaknesses

3. *Course of Action*

What path is most likely to get the team to its goal?
Identify three alternatives. Select one by placing an asterisk beside it.

_____

_____

_____

_____

4. *Develop an Action Plan*

What actions need to be taken, by whom, by when, and with what resources to implement the course of action? Complete the chart on page 68.

5. *Develop Contingency Plans*

What should the team do if the situation changes? List two events that can affect the plan positively and two events that can affect it negatively.

Positive Events	Negative Events

Put an asterisk beside the item that is most likely and most critical.
How will the plan change if this contingency occurs?

_____

_____

TEAM DEVELOPMENT PLAN (FOR ACTION PLAN #4)

EVENT/TASK	PRIMARY PERSON RESPONSIBLE	RESOURCES NEEDED	TARGET COMPLETION DATE	$ BUDGETED	OTHER/NOTES

5. ***The Tools.*** This action plan will use the planning tools discussed in Information Update #3, "Action Planning."

a. Choose one of the tools described in the "Action Planning" information update:

   ▲ Resources checklist

   ▲ Job division

   ▲ Scheduling

      ■ Gantt charting

      ■ PERT charting

b. Make a point to use one (or more) of them the next time you plan an action.

c. During your follow-up discussion on this module, be prepared to tell what happened:

   Briefly describe the goal or situation.

   _____

   _____

   _____

   _____

   What tool did you use? Why did you choose that one?

   _____

   _____

   _____

   _____

   How did it help?

   _____

   _____

   _____

   _____

Evaluation and Follow-Up

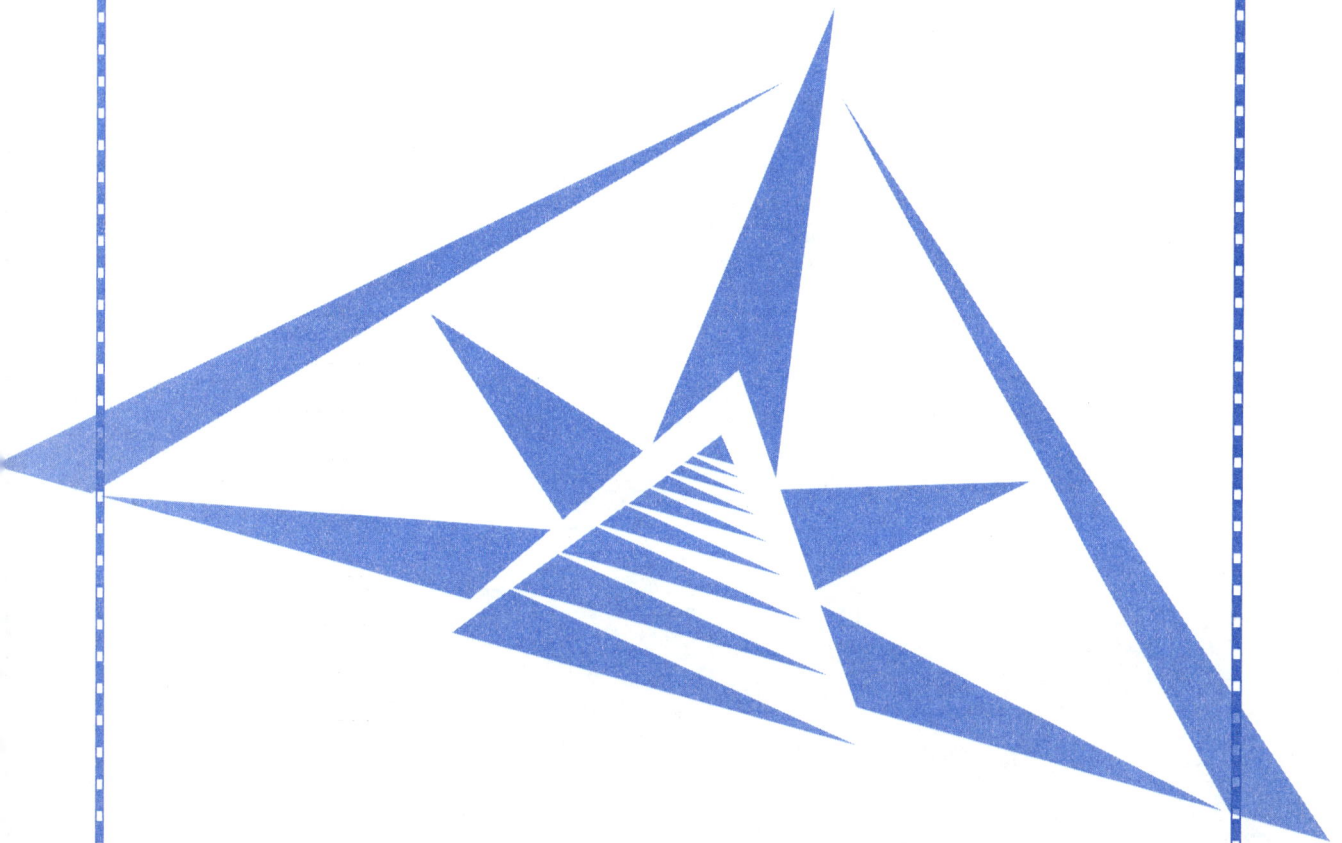

EVALUATION FORM—PLANNING AND GOAL SETTING FOR IMPROVED PERFORMANCE

Directions: The materials in *Planning and Goal Setting for Improved Performance* are designed to help you learn and improve planning and goal setting techniques. After completing all activities in the Participant's Guide, please take a moment to fill out this evaluation form and return it to your course leader. Your input is valuable for ensuring that the training provided meets your needs. We encourage your comments and suggestions.

1. Date of Session _____

2. Location/Business Unit _____

3. Have you taken part in other topics in this Series? Yes _____ No _____

4. The goals and objectives of this module are described in the Introduction on page 1. Do you feel they were met? Yes _____ No _____

  a. If yes, what helped?

  _____

  _____

  b. If no, why were they not met?

  _____

  _____

5. What two things did you like best about this module?

  _____

  _____

6. What two things did you like least about this module?

  _____

  _____

7. What recommendations would you make for conducting this session again?

  _____

  _____

  _____

Index

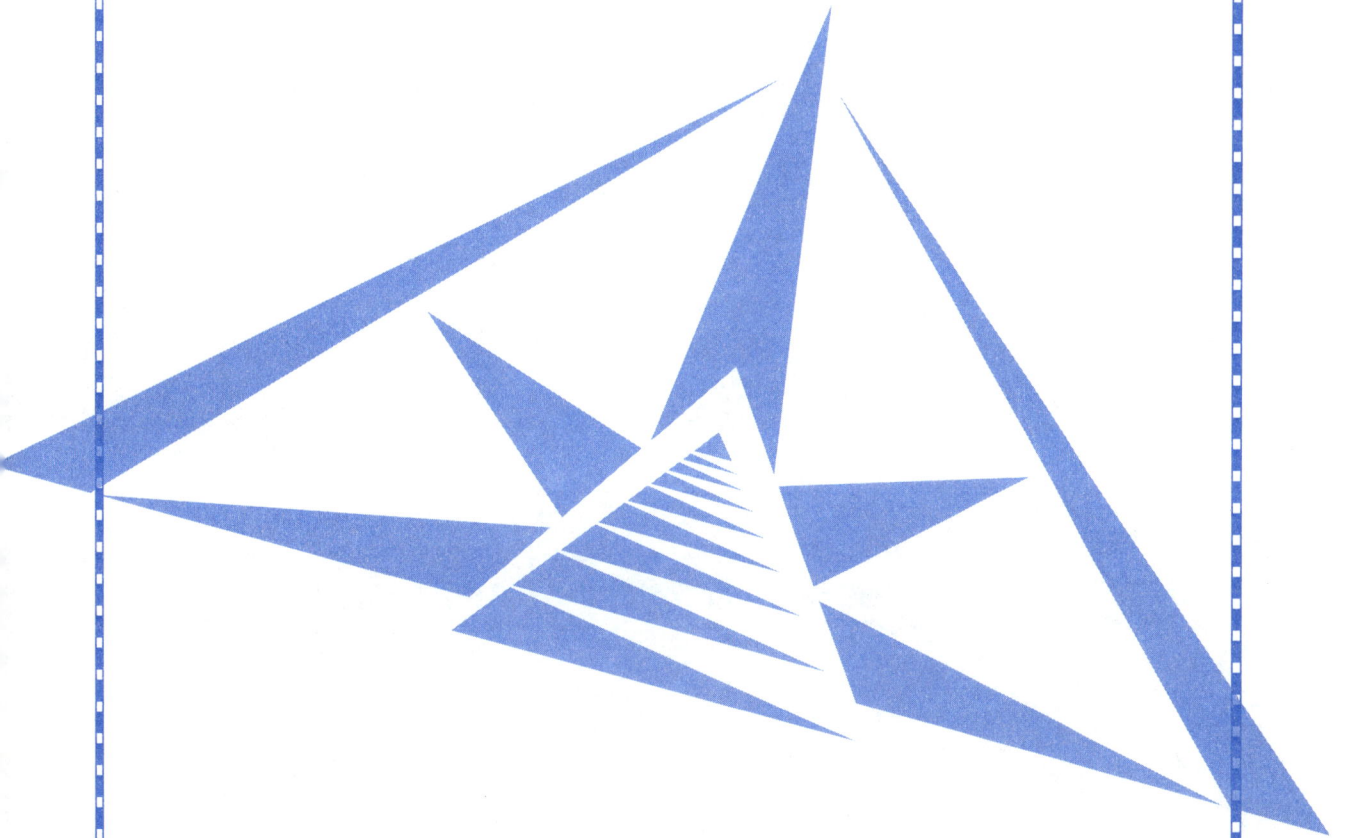

Index

A

A primer on planning, information update #1, 11-16
Action
    plan. *See specific plan.*
        after complete, 36-37
        assessment, 59
        checkpoints, 13
        five-step, 28
        review, 58-60
        step 4 of planning process, 13-14
    planning, information update #3, 27-38
Alicija's plan, application question #4, 47
Application questions. *See specific question.*
Assessment, of action plan, 59

C

Characteristics of sound plan, 16
Checkpoints
    interim, when developing action plan, 13
    review, step 5 of action plan, 28
Charts, Gantt and PERT, 30-33
Contingency plans, 36
    in personal development, 63
    step 5 of planning process, 13-14
    in team development, 67
Critical path, in PERT chart, 30, 33
Current plan review, action plan #2, 58-60

D

Date of completion for action plan, 14
    setting, step 4 of action plan, 28
    target, 27
Debrief plan, step 7 of planning process, 13-14

E

Evaluation
    form, 73
    of plan results, 37

F

Failure, teams failing goals, 43

G

Five-step action plan, 28, 38-39
Form, evaluation, 73

Gantt chart, 30-32
Goals
    direction set, 21-22
    "Harry's aggressive goals", application question #2, 43
    identify, step 1 of planning process, 13-14
    involvement by employees, 21-22
    "Maria's goals", application question #1, 41-42
    problems setting, 41
    "Setting and achieving worthwhile goals", information update #2, 19-23
    S-M-A-R-T, 19-20, 22-23
    subgoals, 20-21
    team, 42
        failing, 43
    timeliness, 22
    "Too many goals", application question #5, 49
    "Your team's S-M-A-R-T goals", 55-57

H

Harry's aggressive goals, application question #2, 43
Hiring time at the firm
    application question #3, 44-46
    Gantt chart, 45
House
    Gantt chart for building, 31
        revised, 34
    PERT chart for building, 32
        revised, 35

I

Implementation of plan, step 6 of planning process, 13-14
Information, collect, step 2 of planning process, 13-14

Information updates. *See specific update.*

J
Job
    dividing, step 2 of action plan, 28
    resources needed, step 3 of action plan,
        28

L
Leadership role, 4

M
Management
    plan as tool, 15, 37
Maria's goals, application question #1, 41-42
Meeting, "The staff meeting", application
        question #6, 49-51
Milestones
    of action plan, 13
    review, step 5 of action plan, 28

O
Objectives, "setting and achieving
        worthwhile goals", information update
        #2, 19-23

P
Paperwork required for goal setting, 47
Path, critical, in PERT chart, 30
Personal
    growth plan, action plan #3, 61-64
    plan development, 62-64
PERT charts, 30-32, 33
    for application question #6, 51
Plan
    action. *See specific plan.*
        checkpoints, 13
        after complete, 36-37
        assessment, 59
        review, 58-60
        step 4 of planning process, 13-14
    "Alicija's plan", application question #4, 47
    attributes of successful, 14-15
    characteristics of sound plan, 16
    contingency, 36
        step 5 of planning process, 13-14
    debriefing, 37

    step 7 of planning process, 13-14
    evaluation of results, 37
    five-step action plan, 28
    implementation, 36-37
        step 6 of planning process, 13-14
    as management tool, 15, 37
    personal development, 62-64
    "Personal growth plan", action plan #3,
        61-64
    road map analogy, 11-12
    strategic, 12
    tactical, 12
    team development, 66-68
    "Team plans", action plan #4, 65-68
Planning process, seven steps, 13-14
Problems with goal setting, 41
Program Evaluation Review Technique
        (PERT), 30-31, 33
Project, minimum time to complete, 33

Q
Questions, application. *See specific question.*

R
Resources
    for completing task, 38
    to do job, step 3 of action plan, 28
Road map, like a plan, 11-12
Roadblocks in planning process, 14
Role of leader, 4
Routes, find alternative, step 3 of planning
        process, 13-14
Rules for successful plan, 13

S
S-M-A-R-T
    acronym for good goal, 19-20, 22-23
    goals, "Your team's S-M-A-R-T goals",
        action plan #1, 55-57
Schedule steps, step 4 of action plan, 28
Self-awareness tool, 7-8
Setting and achieving worthwhile goals,
        information update #2, 19-23
Slack time, in Gantt or PERT chart, 30
Staff meeting, application question #6, 49-51
Steps, seven steps of planning process, 13-14
Strategic plan, 12

Subgoals, 20-21
  with action plan, 14

T
Tactical plan, 12
Task
  identifying, step 1 of action plan, 28
  responsibility, step 2 of action plan, 28
Team
  assessing team goals, 57
  goals, 42
    failure of, 43
  plans
    action plan #4, 65-68

development, 66-68
Time
  minimum to complete project, 33
  for plan, 12
  slack, in Gantt or PERT chart, 30
Timeliness of goal, 22
Too many goals, application question #5, 49
Tool
  management plan, 15, 37
  self-awareness, 7-8
Tools, action plan #5, 69-70

U
Update, information. *See specific update.*

NOTES

NOTES

NOTES

NOTES

NOTES

NOTES

NOTES

NOTES

NOTES